There's A Beach of Gold Just Around the Corner

by

Ali Bagley with Keith Trubshaw

Unlocking Contract Opportunities for SMEs

Aka

Take back your weekends!

Beach of Gold

ISBN: 9781738535828

DEDICATION

For every person in business who understands the difference between cost and investment

ACKNOWLEDGEMENTS

At Kindridge Bid Solutions, we are more of a family than just colleagues. We have each other's backs; we support and work for each other, not just with each other.

So, the first person we acknowledge is Sarah Cowell, the cog in the wheel that keeps everything turning.

Then we thank all of those people we have met and worked with over our combined almost 100 years of experience. Those who inspired us and led us, as well as those who frankly made our lives hell but, in doing so, taught us how not to do things.

And, of course, the families and friends we spend our time with, time we cherish and make possible by practising what we preach in the pages of this book.

CONTENTS

FOREWORD

By Keith Trubshaw

Does anyone ever read the forward of a book? If I said that I always do; I'd be telling a lie.

I'm usually too eager to get to the meat and potatoes of what I might learn. If you like, I want to know 'what's in it for me!'

Well, in the hope that you do, in fact, read the forward of this particular book, here's a taste of what you will find within its pages. It's a very short taste but profound, nonetheless:

- If you are in a business that must compete in markets where there is substantial competition.
- If you know that there are wonderful opportunities out there, if only you could tap into them.
- If you could only develop the skills you need without investing £1,000s in training,
- If you understand the power of learning from experts instead of wasting time and money learning from mistakes, then this book is for you.

It will show you how to find lucrative opportunities and then how to grow your skills, knowledge and expertise to bid for them in a way that maximises your chance of success.

Take a seat and enjoy the ride. It might be a bit bumpy, but it's going to be very worth your while.

BEFORE WE BEGIN

Keiths' introduction

Recognising the Dilemma

Let's start with a question: what is the cruellest four-letter word in the English language? Before you go off into a world of expletives, let me tell you the answer. The word is time!

It is too often ignored, and it is the scarcest, most abused gift that we are given. To those of us who work in the world of business, time is our master.

Our goals are set in terms of money, fame, or status, but the one thing we need to achieve those goals is this four-letter word:

Time.

If I had more time, I would...

If I had more time, I could...

If we only had more time, we could...

You fill in the blanks.

Even if I have no physics skills, if you give me enough time, I will build a rocket to take you to the moon or a Tardis to take you to the other side of the universe. Anything is possible, given enough time. This book is not so much about finding but leveraging time. Increasing your

Tendering or bidding know-how without wasting time on making mistakes and combining this with that leveraged time to maximise your chances of success.

How many times do we hear? 'I'd like to, but I don't have time', often coming from our own lips. Or 'I can't afford the time'. Here's the thing: when a slice of an annual £290 billion public sector contracts market is there for the taking; we should actually be saying, 'I can't afford NOT to take the time.'

But there is a dilemma here. It's a dilemma faced by every owner or manager of a business.

'Where is my time best spent? Should I work on things I know will make The company money? Or should I be chasing rainbows?'

In a way, the answer is both. We cannot afford (in the short term at least) to take our hands off the tiller for even a moment.

By taking our focus from what we know we are good at, those things that we know make us money and help us pay the wages we are putting the business at risk.

Who in their right mind would want to do that?

One way to solve this dichotomy is to throw more hours into the working day. 9 to 5, becomes 8 to 6, or 7 to 7, the list goes on. We spend ever-increasing hours on the day job, sometimes just to keep our head above water. Then we come home, eat a quick meal, shout at the kids, and start working on some crazy idea that we might, just might, win a huge slice of business. Will we win it? Do we stand any chance at all, or are we just chasing those rainbows?

The bidding process demands focus, time and effort. It is not something that can be done by someone who is worn out by having spent too many hours at the corporate grindstone. That's a sure road to failure and a very expensive failure at that.

If we are going to pick up any of the nuggets from the Beach of Gold we sit on; we need to give it our best shot. We need to let go of the day-to-day business whilst we concentrate on the big prize. Trust me, I've been there many times; I know how hard that can be.

The promise of this book is that it will show you that there are ways to manage the bidding process. Ways to set yourself up for success without driving yourself into an early grave or putting your company at risk.

Good luck, and here's to your success.

Alis' introduction

The Journey Ahead

As Keith says, 'The bidding process demands focus, time and effort. It is not something that can be done by someone who is worn out by having spent too many hours at the corporate grindstone'.

Yet you sit in that 'Lonely Seat'. You know that the business rises or falls with you. And so, you work and work, miss the weekends, the family time, the nights out with friends, the holidays. You can't let go; you have to constantly tend to the activity and responsibilities your position has given you.

There is another way you know . . .

Do you want your weekends back and be safe in the knowledge that your business is flourishing? Do you want to have the security of long-term contracts, delivered by you and your growing team, ensuring that the business thrives? Of course you do.

Now, to achieve this, you are going to have to invest some time, trust and money. Nothing worth having is free, is it?

Your journey begins now, with you committing the time needed to read and absorb the nuggets of gold in this book.

When you do that, you will be on a pathway to learning how to take back your time, grow your business and secure your future.

I suggest bite-sized chunks to begin with. Set aside 15 minutes a day to read a chapter or part of a chapter. You can find 15 minutes yes? Here's a tip: take the book to the loo with you, no one is going to disturb you, and you have to go anyway . . .

Our chapters are written in a 'one follows on from the other' kind of order however, once you have read them once, you can dip in and out of the ones you need for reference in any order you want. This little book is going to be your bidding handbook for quite a while.

Here's to our journey together.

AN EXPLANATION OF TERMS AND ACRONYMS

Also, before we begin, a few things you may need clarity on . . .

Term / Acronym	Meaning
Tender:	A formal invitation or solicitation, usually issued by a company, organisation, or government agency, inviting bids or proposals from qualified contractors or suppliers to provide goods or services.
	Tenders typically outline the requirements, specifications, terms, and conditions for the project or contract being offered.
	Bidders interested in securing the work submit their proposals or bids in response to the tender.
	The selection process may involve evaluating factors such as price, quality, experience, capabilities, and compliance with the tender requirements. Ultimately, the tendering process aims to ensure transparency, fairness, and competitiveness in awarding contracts or projects.
Technical Response:	The section of your response to a tender which typically includes the quality questions and questions relating to your delivery and expertise.
Specification:	The part of the tender which outlines what the client is looking for from potential bidders.
ITT (Invitation To Tender):	A formal document issued by a company, organisation or government agency to invite qualified suppliers, contractors, or service providers to submit bids or proposals for a specific project or contract.
	The ITT outlines the details and requirements of the project, including scope of work, specifications, terms and conditions, deadlines,

	evaluation criteria, and any other pertinent information that prospective bidders need to know in order to prepare their bids.
	The purpose of an invitation to tender is to attract competitive bids from eligible vendors and to ensure that the selection process is fair, transparent, and based on predefined criteria.
	Once the bids are submitted, the issuing party evaluates them according to the specified criteria and selects the most suitable bidder to fulfil the project or contract requirements.
RFP / RFQ (Request for Proposal or Quotation)	Similar to an ITT but typically allows for more flexibility and creativity in the proposals submitted by vendors.
	The RFP outlines the project's objectives, scope of work, desired outcomes, evaluation criteria, deadlines, terms and conditions, and any other relevant information that prospective bidders need to know in order to prepare their proposals.
	Once the RFP is issued, interested vendors or service providers submit their proposals, detailing how they intend to meet the requirements outlined in the document. The issuing party evaluates the proposals based on predefined criteria and may engage in negotiations with the bidders before selecting the most suitable proposal to fulfil the project's needs.
PQQ (Pre-Qualification Questionnaire)	The purpose of a PQQ is to pre-screen potential suppliers or contractors before inviting them to participate in the tender or bidding process.
	The PQQ typically includes questions related to the supplier's or contractor's capabilities, experience, financial stability, technical expertise, qualifications, certifications, and any other relevant information that the buyer deems

	necessary to assess the suitability of the potential suppliers.
	The responses to the PQQ help the buyer or contracting authority to shortlist qualified suppliers who meet the minimum criteria for participating in the tender process. Only those suppliers who successfully pass the pre-qualification stage by providing satisfactory responses to the PQQ are invited to submit formal bids or proposals in response to the tender or invitation to tender (ITT).
	Proposal The Proposal is your response to an ITT or RFQ, detailing your offer, solution and price for the work tendered.
Procurement:	In the context of bidding, procurement refers to the process of acquiring goods, services, or works from an external source, typically through a formal purchasing process.
	It involves the identification of needs, sourcing of suppliers or contractors, negotiation of terms and conditions, and ultimately, the selection and acquisition of the desired goods, services, or works.
	Procurement activities often include:
	Identifying Requirements: Determining the specific needs and requirements of the organisation or project.
	Sourcing Suppliers: Researching and identifying potential suppliers, contractors, or vendors who can meet the requirements.
	Issuing Tender Documents: This includes preparing and issuing tender documents such as invitations to tender (ITT), requests for proposal (RFP) or pre-qualification questionnaires (PQQ) to solicit bids or proposals from interested parties.
	Evaluating Bids or Proposals: Reviewing and

	evaluating the bids or proposals submitted by suppliers or contractors based on predefined criteria such as price, quality, experience, and compliance with specifications.
	Negotiating Contracts: Engaging in negotiations with selected suppliers or contractors to finalise terms and conditions, including pricing, delivery schedules, warranties, and other relevant factors.
	Awarding Contracts: Selecting the most suitable supplier or contractor, and awarding the contract based on the evaluation criteria and negotiations.
	Managing Contracts: Overseeing and managing the execution of contracts, including monitoring supplier performance, ensuring compliance with terms and conditions, and resolving any issues or disputes that may arise during the contract period.
	Effective procurement practices play a crucial role in ensuring that organisations obtain the best value for money, minimise risks and achieve their objectives efficiently and effectively.
	Bidding is an integral part of the procurement process, as it allows suppliers and contractors to compete for contracts by submitting competitive bids or proposals in response to procurement opportunities.
LA (Local Authority)	A governmental body responsible for the administration of local government functions and services within a specific geographic area.
	Local authorities operate at different levels, including county councils, district councils, borough councils, city councils, and unitary authorities, depending on the structure of local government in a particular area.
	Local authorities are responsible for delivering a

	wide range of public services and functions for which they may issue ITTs/RFQs including:
	• Education
	• Social Services
	• Housing
	• Planning and Development
	• Transportation
	• Waste Management
	• Environmental Health
	• Leisure and Recreation
	Local authorities derive their powers and responsibilities from legislation enacted by the UK Parliament and operate within the framework of national laws and regulations.
	They are accountable to local residents and elected councillors who represent the interests of the community.
Public Sector:	That part of the economy in which goods and services are provided by the government or government-controlled entities rather than by private companies or individuals. It encompasses a wide range of organisations and activities that are funded and operated by government entities at various levels, including local, regional, national, and international levels.
	Key characteristics of the public sector include:
	• Government Control
	• Public Ownership
	• Service Provision
	• Funding
	• Regulation and Oversight
	• Accountability and Transparency
	Examples of entities and activities within the public sector include government departments, ministries, local authorities, public schools,

	public hospitals, public transportation systems, law enforcement agencies, regulatory bodies, and public utilities such as water and electricity providers. Overall, the public sector plays a vital role in promoting social equity, economic development, and the general welfare of society by providing essential services and infrastructure that benefit the population as a whole.
Private Sector:	That part of the economy in which goods and services are produced and distributed by privately owned businesses or organisations rather than by government entities. It encompasses a wide range of enterprises operating in various industries and sectors, including manufacturing, finance, retail, technology, healthcare, and services. Key characteristics of the private sector include: • Private Ownership • Profit Orientation • Market-driven Economy • Entrepreneurship and Innovation • Employment Generation • Risk and Competition • Financial Markets Overall, the private sector plays a crucial role in driving economic growth, wealth creation and innovation, contributing to the prosperity and development of societies around the world. It complements the public sector by providing goods, services, employment opportunities, and investment opportunities that contribute to the overall well-being and advancement of communities and nations.
Case Study:	In the context of bidding for contracts, a "case study" refers to a detailed analysis or example

that demonstrates a bidder's previous experience, capabilities, and success in delivering similar projects or contracts. Case studies are often included as part of a bid proposal to showcase the bidder's expertise, track record, and ability to meet the requirements and expectations of the client.

Key elements of a case study in the context of bidding for contracts include:

• Project Description: A description of the specific project or contract that was undertaken by the bidder, including its scope, objectives, and key deliverables.

• Client Information: Information about the client or organisation for whom the project was completed, including their industry, sector, and any relevant background information.

• Challenges and Solutions: Identification of any challenges, obstacles, or complexities encountered during the project, along with the strategies, solutions, and approaches employed to overcome them.

• Methodology and Approach: An explanation of the methodologies, techniques and approaches used by the bidder to execute the project and achieve the desired outcomes.

• Results and Achievements: A summary of the results, achievements, and outcomes of the project, including measurable metrics, key performance indicators, and any notable successes or benefits realised by the client.

• Client Testimonials or References: Testimonials, feedback, or references from the client or stakeholders involved in the project, attesting to the bidder's performance, quality of work, and professionalism.

• Relevance to Current Bid: Demonstrating how

	the experience and lessons learned from the case study are relevant and applicable to the current bid or project being pursued.
	Including case studies in a bid proposal helps to provide concrete evidence of the bidder's capabilities, credibility, and suitability for the contract being sought.
	By showcasing successful past projects and demonstrating the ability to deliver results, case studies can significantly strengthen the bidder's overall bid, and increase their chances of winning the contract.
Proposal or Bid:	Your response to the ITT or RFQ issued by the purchasing client or their procurement agent.

Beach of Gold

CHAPTER 1: THE CONUNDRUM OF STAGNATION

Introduction

Any business that isn't growing is not standing still; it's going backwards.

The Mid-Sized Business Stalemate

You are standing at a junction, a junction that offers potential for growth, yet presents challenges in gathering the necessary resources to support that growth.

Imagine this scenario:

You know a contract is available for bidding, and you have the necessary resources to deliver it well. However, you lack the expertise to create a winning proposal. Despite this obstacle, you are determined to proceed. You invest significant time and effort into the endeavour, only to be defeated by a competitor who is slightly more advanced in their development.

You stressed about it, went for it anyway (where there's a will, there's a way), spent hours of time and effort doing your best, and then lost out to a competitor who is just a bit further on in their growth than you are.

Now, that has cost you money and left you frustrated, disheartened, and in trouble for missing family events because you were writing technical responses until midnight every weekend.

Best just to carry on networking and hope to pick up sales that Way?

Wrong.

The truth is, this entire situation has not only failed to advance your business, but it has also caused you to regress in terms of both time and money.

Now, here's the solution you need to make that growth happen.

We offer you the following options, each with the potential to catalyse growth. Regardless of which path you choose, it's important to take action and make a decision that aligns with your goals and objectives.

Option 1

Dedicate some of your time and effort to perusing the contents of this book. Within its pages, you will discover guidance and resources to enhance your abilities and proficiency in crafting successful bid responses.

Whilst it may not transform you into an expert, you will emerge more knowledgeable, prepared to embark on the next phase of your development, and so able to spend less time and energy on bidding.

If when you have read this book, you decide you don't want to go it alone, there are another couple of options:

Option 2

Collaborate with a seasoned bid consultant to create compelling and successful contract proposals, allowing you to focus on your business and home life responsibilities, like actually turning up to your kids' swimming gala. We call this the SOD principle, getting the S*** Off your

Desk!

A specialist external bid consultant takes care of the time-consuming and complex task of bid development, doing it faster and more efficiently than you could, increasing your chances of securing the contracts you want. Whilst this requires an investment, it's a smart decision that may ultimately save your precious resources and improve your business's prospects.

Option 3

Consider investing in the development of your team's bidding skills by bringing in an expert trainer to provide comprehensive knowledge, process and writing coaching. Although this may require temporarily diverting staff from their regular duties and requires some upfront expense, the long-term benefits of having an in-house team capable of crafting successful bids can far outweigh the costs.

This investment can lead to increased efficiency and profitability in the long run, as well as enhance your company's overall competitiveness in the market. Additionally, having a trained team will allow you to tackle future bids with confidence and improved chances of success.

As an addendum, or Option 4, you can always access online training for you and your team to learn the basics and get started on your own. Try this one on for size:

https://alibagleycoach.samcart.com/products/an-introduction-to-bidding

The Urgency of Seeking New Avenues

In the fast-paced world of business, we are constantly seeking ways to maximise growth and profitability. Bidding for work can be a promising strategy for expanding business horizons, but it raises concerns about the potential impact on day-to-day operations. In our 'Is Your Business Growth Ready'? Quiz, we delved into this very topic, and the results shed light on perceptions surrounding bidding work.

The survey revealed that 57% of respondents believed that bidding work adds to their day-to-day workload, whilst 29% disagreed, and 14% were undecided. These numbers offer a glimpse into the various perspectives held by business professionals when it comes to the impact of bidding on their daily tasks.

1. The Perception of Added Workload:

The majority of respondents felt that bidding work indeed increases their day-to-day workload. This sentiment is likely rooted in the additional time and effort required to prepare bids, research potential clients, and tailor proposals to meet specific requirements. It also highlights the challenges of balancing bid work with ongoing operations and existing commitments.

2. Factors Influencing Workload Impact:

The perception of bidding adding to workload can vary based on several factors. The size and resources of the organisation, the complexity of the bidding process, and the availability of dedicated staff to handle bid-related tasks can significantly influence the perceived impact. Smaller businesses with limited resources may feel the burden more intensely compared to larger corporations.

3. The Potential for Efficient Bidding Strategies:

Whilst bidding work may contribute to daily workload, it's crucial to recognise that implementing efficient bidding strategies can help mitigate this impact. Adopting effective tools, streamlining processes and allocating dedicated resources to handle bid-related tasks can optimise efficiency and reduce the strain on day-to-day operations.

The survey results highlight a divided perspective on whether bidding work adds to the daily workload. It is crucial for businesses to acknowledge the potential impact and challenges associated with bidding for their organisation, whilst also understanding that strategic approaches and efficient practices can help alleviate the burden. By harnessing the power of winning bid strategies, entrepreneurs can supercharge their business growth and unlock new opportunities.

Finding those opportunities

You know that you want and need to grow as a business. And that means constantly seeking new avenues; in fact, you probably spend most of your working day doing just that (plus the other 101 things the boss has to do!).

So, the first thing we are going to look at is where to find those contracts that a) you can win and b) you can deliver.

Nope, hold the front door. First, we have to get your bid ready!

Keith's insight from the Lonely Seat

It's an age-old question. Should I be working on the business or in the business?

We all know the answer, but chances are that few of us manage to get past the first phone call or email of the day. Who was it that said the best-laid plans always fall down after the first punch in the mouth?

Short-term firefighting vs. Long-term strategy is an ever-present dilemma. Planning for a better tomorrow is a constant battle with "short-term firefighting", usually winning by a considerable margin.

Equipping our organisation to be bid-ready and capable of tendering for work we might have thought out of reach falls squarely into the long-term strategy category. Yet the rewards can be exponential, not just in the long term but in the medium and maybe even in the short term, too. The challenge is finding the time to take our noses from the grindstone so that we can look to the horizon.

If we succeed, the business can be transformed into a success story. But here's the thing: not only will our business be better off financially, but engaging the staff in the bidding process will substantially increase their involvement and caring about the business. They will have their eyes on the horizon. The team spirit that can be engendered by helping employees see the long-term picture, and knowing they are part of going for it, is incalculable.

Beach of Gold

Beach of Gold

CHAPTER 2: TIME AS THE TRUE CURRENCY

AKA spend time in preparation so as not to waste time later down the track.

Introduction

We have been doing a bit of research into our clients and contacts 'bid readiness' via our conversations as well as collecting data from our scorecard, 'Supercharge Your Business Growth Quiz'.

The results we are going to focus on first are what we discovered around two key questions:

The results show that most of our responders are just not bid ready yet. Certainly not in terms of having the collateral to evidence their ability to deliver.

Very few have any kind of evidence to use to demonstrate their track record or ability to deliver, and that is a 'fail' when it comes to securing contracts via tender.

Plus, there are so many other elements you need to have in place, but we will look at those later.

The MD's Quest for Efficiency

Whether you are relying solely on yourself or have a small group working alongside you, or even if you hold a position of leadership within a large corporate department, the reality is that both your time and the time of your team will inevitably be dedicated to the operation and provision of your business's services or products.

Ensuring that your organisation operates efficiently is crucial, and dedicating time and resources to bidding can have a significant impact on productivity. However, it's important to consider the potential benefits of investing in preparing evidential collateral, as this will lead to increased success in bids and ultimately, improved business outcomes.

Balancing these competing demands can be challenging, and it's essential to carefully weigh the opportunity costs before making a decision. Unless you have the fundamental components in place prior to tendering, you'll be headed down a dead-end road.

Speaking to a procurement lead recently, we inquired about the three main requirements local authorities have for suppliers when bidding for contracts. Here is the summarised response:

1. **Social validation,** providing proof, evidence, and testimonials that showcase your delivery methods and successful, measurable outcomes.
2. **Social value,** demonstrating how your actions and approaches benefit the community, its residents, and other businesses.
3. **Environmental impact**, such as detailing your progress towards achieving carbon neutrality, including your starting point, targets, initiatives, and positive effects on the local

environment.

It is essential to have all this information documented, along with case studies, client testimonials, certifications, accreditations, and key performance indicators (KPIs) that serve as concrete evidence of the positive impact your business contributes.

Your prospective clients have their own objectives and performance metrics to meet, and it's crucial that your contract delivery aligns with and supports their goals. To ensure your team's ability to submit proof of being able to efficiently deliver the contract, you may need to streamline their processes and provide them with the necessary resources and time to develop the required collateral.

There are ten top things you need to do or have in place before you even begin to start looking for contract opportunities:

1 **Plan tendering into your business strategy**
What level of income from contracts do you want to achieve and what will the investment be? What resources do you need to deliver that level of contracts?

2 **Know your skills**
Do you know how to dissect a tender? Write winning responses? Or do you need support or training for that?

3 **Know what the clients problem is**
Any bid you submit must demonstrate that you both understand the clients problem and how you are going to solve it (to time and budget).

4 **Evidence**
For any tender you must be able to evidence that you can deliver what the client is tendering for. And really know what they are tendering for!

5 **More Evidence**
Almost all bids will need to include case studies. These are stories about specific projects, products or activities you have carried out that relate to what is being asked for on the contract being tendered. Similar value / client / outputs.

6 **Social Value**
You will need to build a library of evidence of social value. That is business activity that has benefitted your local community or charities.

7 **Environment and Sustainability**
Critical to almost every bid is to be able to prove how your services, products and/or operations are environmentally friendly and sustainable. i.e., your strategy to achieve net zero, how you deal with waste etc.

8 **Resources**
Do you have the right people in place, and can you evidence their skills and qualifications in terms of the delivery of any contract you are bidding for? Thinking you can recruit IF you win will not be acceptable to potential clients.

9 **Know what's coming**
Deciding to submit a bid only when the tender is released, without building relationships and doing research is risky.

10 **Can you afford to invest?**
Bidding is expensive. Use experts if you don't know how or you will be throwing your money and time away.

Strategies to Reclaim Valuable Time

We can't make more time, but we can find ways to use what we have more effectively. Whether you are a one-man band or have team support, here are a few ways to streamline your operations to create opportunities for the bid preparation work you know needs to be done.

Delegate

Who in your team can do some of the work that you do to free you up to lead, manage or write bids? Really think about this.

So many of us are guilty of assuming that no one can do what we do, as well as we can do it, or that it will take as long to explain it as it would to do it yourself.

Delegation is an incredibly effective tool for upskilling your team, ensuring they have the knowledge and skills to keep things going when you are out of action. Promoting this kind of growth also builds trust and teamwork, so essential for any business to flourish.

Right Resource, right task

So, try this exercise:

List your team members, both those employed by you and those you outsource work to. Write a list of their individual skills. Then, write down why you employed them:

Team Member	Their Skills	Why You Employed Them
Name:	1. 2. 3. 4. 5.	
Name:	1. 2. 3. 4. 5.	

Name:	1.	
	2.	
	3.	
	4.	
	5.	
Name:	1.	
	2.	
	3.	
	4.	
	5.	

Now think about each individual, and in the left-hand column of the table below, write down all the tasks and activities you do yourself on a regular basis. Then note against each task a resource or resources who could do that for you, for their growth as much as to give you more time:

Task / Activity	Resource to Delegate to
1.	
2.	
3.	
4.	

Beach of Gold

5.	

If you think there is nothing you can delegate after this exercise, then you are beyond help, my friend! Yes, it may take a little time to hand things over effectively and require a level of trust. But you employed them for a reason, right?

Delegation is an art, and identifying the right resource for each task is key to its success.

For the One-Man (Woman)-Band

No team to delegate to, so what can you do?

Outsource or employ?

Again, we are talking about investment; outsourcing or employing will attach a cost to your business. However, this investment can significantly repay itself in terms of what you can achieve in the time freed up by the extra resources you invest in.

Let me give you a scenario around this in terms of facts and figures:

You are a solopreneur service provider. Let's say you deliver first-aid training to organisations. You carry out 4-hour or 8-hour sessions, and you charge £100 an hour for that service.

One day a week, you keep free to do your accounts, admin, invoicing, social media, marketing emails etc. In effect, that costs your business £800 in lost revenue because you can't be in two places at once.

Add to this the fact that admin and marketing are not really your forte. It probably takes you twice as long to do a good job of it as it would a professional. And won't ever be done as well as they can do it.

So, you spend an entire day on admin at a cost to your business in lost revenue of £800. Ah ha, you say, No, I do the admin in the evening and at weekends when I wouldn't be out delivering training so there is no lost revenue.

Ah ha, we say, but what about the lost hours with your friends and family, resting up so you can be on your best game next week or tomorrow; what are you losing in those hours other than money?

So, back to our sums.

You decide to outsource your administration (invoicing, finances, filing, record keeping, etc.) A good administrator can easily cover that in 3 hours a week for a solopreneur.

They charge you £30 an hour. You decide to outsource your marketing (social media, email campaigns, lead generation, newsletter production, etc.) A good marketer can cover that in 3 hours a week. They charge you £40 an hour.

Your total weekly outlay for both services is £210. You can now take on extra training work (and you will get more because that's what a marketer will get for you) at £800 a day. You are up £590 a week, approximately £2,500 a month.

You might choose to use that day to prepare bids for contracts to grow your business, using the tips and tools in this book. Or use the spare £2,500 a month as your bid budget and engage a professional to win you more work, which will facilitate more business, more income, the growth of a team . . .

One final tip. Look into employment schemes that enable you to take on help (such as an apprentice, etc) that is government funded.

It's super win-win, that one.

Prioritise

So, now you have identified a few tasks that can be passed to others and you now have a bit more time in the bank. The next thing you can do is look at your remaining tasks and prioritise them.

There is a rule of three here:

1. What must be done now
2. What can be done later
3. What can be left until you have time or be passed to others

Your priority is, of course, the first: What must be done now? List your day-to-day tasks first and your stand-alone tasks second.

Task	Action: Do Now / Do Later / Delegate	Time Required
1.		
2.		

3.		
4.		
5.		
6.		
7.		
8.		

Use this list to identify what is important and put a time duration next to it. If you can delegate it, that is time you are saving to work on growing your business.

So now I hope you have had a good think about the benefits of delegation and prioritisation and the financial benefits and time-saving opportunities that this will bring you.

Keith's insight from the Lonely Seat

What Ali has written about here boils down to the age-old question...

"How do we get a pint from a half-pint pot?"

The obvious answer of course - you can't. But actually, that's not quite true. Where does it say in the rules that we can't use the half-pint pot twice or any number of times? And that's just what delegation is. It refills as many pots as we like, provided we accept the fact that we will be using smaller pots to do it. So, how does that analogy fit in with delegation?

The most challenging obstacle we face when we contemplate delegation is trust. Do we trust (in this case, our half-pint pot) to do the job as well as we would? How can they? They're not the boss. But the fact is, they may not be as good as us, but they will have more time to devote to getting the job done properly.

You are the pint-pot that could've done the job in one go if you'd only had time. It might take them several trips to fill the vessel, but the result would be the same. And here's the kicker: the task will have freed you up to work on other things that make the business more successful. So, in summary, trust the half-pint pots to get the job done. It might take them longer, but at least they'll complete it.

Beach of Gold

Beach of Gold

CHAPTER 3: OUTSOURCING YOUR BIDDING AND CUTTING CORNERS

To paraphrase Nanny McPhee:

'When you need us, but do not want us, we are there for you. When you want us, but no longer need us then we have done what we set out to do'.

Introduction

We are nipping back to Options 2 and 3 here: Collaboration with a seasoned external bid consultant for your bidding work and/or training your team.

You may have already experienced the benefits of outsourcing or delegating in terms of your daily workload. Using the same principles, think about the benefits of outsourcing your bidding work.

Plus, we thought it might save you some time to know a bit more about what a specialist can do for you right off the bat to save you spending time reading the whole book and then deciding you don't want the hassle of bidding yourself after all.

Weighing the Pros and Cons

In essence the pros are all about having a virtual expert team at your fingertips that save you time and effort by doing the work for you. The cons, just 1, the financial outlay (and maybe some resource time to provide information).

Crafting a Balanced Approach

The key here is to think very carefully about the cost in time and resources required to do it yourself, plotted against the level of risk of that action, versus the price of a consultant and the increased possibility of success that brings with it. Because both options are going to require investment.

Developing Your Collateral

We have already given you the ten top tips for getting bid ready so let's go into that in a bit more depth.

The activity of gathering information, developing materials and building prospective client relationships is known in the trade as 'Capture Planning'.

You will be capturing the necessary information and tools you need as well as growing your understanding of your target client and market. Looking at your competition also falls into the area of capture planning.

1. Plan tendering into your business strategy

What level of income from contracts do you want to achieve and what will the investment be? What resources do you need to deliver that level of contracts?

This is about forecasting your potential income against costs and making sure you have the resources in place to generate that income.

If that income generation is going to include resource time of hire of external bid specialists, then this has to be planned into your strategy as a cost. Making an assumption that bidding costs are going to be approximately 10% of the potential income from winning the bid is a good place to start (not 10% of the profit, 10% of the full value!).

Contract value £100,000.00 = cost to bid £10,000. Therefore, be sure that your profit margin from winning the work is at least 10% or over: i.e., your delivery costs are less than £90,000.00 or the bid is not worth winning.

Of course, the financial gain is not the only consideration. You might be happy to break even or make a small loss if the contract moves you into a new marketplace or enhances your reputation and experience for future contract bids.

As you become better at bidding and continue to develop your collateral the costs will come down.

2. Know your skills

Do you know how to dissect a tender? Write winning responses? Understand a specification?

If you don't know what you're doing, the chances of winning a bid are very remote unless it's assessed entirely on price and your bid is the lowest priced!

This book is going to upskill you unless you have already been successfully bidding for a while (but then if that's the case why are you reading it?). You will learn about preparation, dissection, storyboarding, writing techniques and more here (actually even if you have been bidding successfully for a while so read on!).

You can of course enhance your skills with training. There are lots of providers who will come into your workplace and upskill you and your teams, courses you can do online and one to one training that you can get.

The important thing to note here is that bid writing and bid management is a skill and a necessary one to stand any chance of winning.

3. Know what the clients problem is

Any bid you submit must demonstrate that you both understand the clients problem and how you are going to solve it (to time and budget).

This is about market research and relationship building. It is probably the most important part of capture planning for effective bid response development because successful bids are not about what you can do, but about what you can do for them. So, you have to know what they want.

Here are a few pointers for things to be on the lookout for in terms of understanding the needs of prospective clients:

- They like to work with people they know, like and trust so, find out who the decision makers are, where do they network/hangout, be there to get to know them and for them to get to know you.

- Watch for news and information on their web pages and read their strategy documents and forecasts if they are published (public sector bodies will have all this on their website).
- Go along to open council meetings and Local Enterprise Partnership meetings to be seen and to meet members and find out what their plans are and what they need.
- Find their core values / principles, again usually on their websites, so that your responses to their tenders will align with them.
- Be a presence at trade shows, fairs and events. Be seen and talk to people. Offer to come and speak about your business or topical issues you are well versed in, at public sector events.
- Keep an eye on your competition. Look at their press pages, blogs and articles to see where they are hanging out and what they are doing. Be where they are too.

The outcome of this activity will better place you to not only be known by prospective clients but also give you the opportunity to find out, first hand, what keeps them awake at night and what their drivers are. This is gold dust when it comes to drafting a bid response.

4. Evidence

For any tender you must be able to evidence that you can deliver what the client is tendering for. And really know what they are tendering for!

All bids, without exception will expect you to back up whatever you are saying in response to the tender questions, with evidence. Solid, statistic based, validated evidence. This means that to be bid ready you have to have a library of evidence to demonstrate that you are the best business to deliver the contract.

You can't say, 'we have the required number of lorries and drivers in our fleet to fulfil the requirements of the contract'. That's crap, even if the question is, 'do you have the required number of lorries and drivers to deliver the contract requirements?'

You answer should consider why they need that many, what benefits will your numbers provide, where and how you have delivered that successfully in the past and can provide security of promise to meet deadlines in the future. Of course, word count restrictions will come into play but how about something like this:

'We understand the critical importance of meeting delivery deadlines and share your commitment to reliability. Our tailored solution, bespoke to your needs and tried and tested with our existing clients over 20 years, ensures seamless operations to meet and exceed your expectations.

Key Components of Our Proposal:

Fleet Capability:

We commit to providing 10 lorries dedicated to your deliveries.

Our modern fleet is well-maintained, equipped with GPS tracking for real-time monitoring, and meets all safety standards.

Driver Availability:

We have a team of skilled and licensed drivers available 7 days a week.

Our drivers are experienced in efficient route planning and are committed to timely deliveries.

Operational Excellence:

We employ advanced logistics management systems to optimise routes, minimise delays, and enhance efficiency.

Our operations team will proactively address any potential issues to ensure a smooth delivery process.

Communication and Transparency:

You will have access to real-time tracking and regular updates on the status of your deliveries.

Our customer support team is available around the clock to address any queries or concerns.

Flexibility:

We understand the dynamic nature of your industry and can adapt our schedules to accommodate peak periods or urgent requirements.

Only last month we made sure that 3 extra vehicles and drivers were made available from our pool to support an emergency delivery which meant that the client did not have to pay late delivery penalties.

"We were so delighted with RentaLorry being able to jump to and save the day, not to mention £'s in penalties. We would recommend them to any retailer as a delivery company of choice." Ted Theboss, Craftysuppliescostless Ltd.

Service Level Agreements (SLAs):

We propose to establish clear SLAs to define performance expectations, ensuring mutual understanding and accountability.

Benefits of Choosing Us:

- *Proven track record of on-time deliveries.*
- *Comprehensive insurance coverage for goods in transit.*
- *Competitive pricing tailored to your specific requirements.*
- *Dedicated account management for personalized service.*

You see what a difference that makes. You are talking to the clients core need of being able to rely on deliveries being made on time and as efficiently as possible as well as within all of the legal and safety requirements (which you have demonstrated you understand and have in place).

Now you can easily develop that kind of response if you have certain things in place, that you can easily find:

- Insurance documentation
- Testimonials

- Prior knowledge of the clients requirements beyond what is stayed in the specification or the question
- Understanding not just what you deliver but the benefits that gives the client
- Case studies, see point 5

5. More Evidence

Almost all bids will need to include case studies. These are stories about specific projects, products or activities you have carried out that relate to what is being asked for on the contract being tendered. Similar value / client / outputs.

Every time you deliver a contract create a case study that you can use in bids to demonstrate successful contract delivery in the past.

In the context of bidding for contracts, a 'case study' refers to a detailed analysis or example that demonstrates a bidder's previous experience, capabilities, and success in delivering similar projects or contracts. Case studies are often included as part of a bid proposal to showcase the bidder's expertise, track record, and ability to meet the requirements and expectations of the client.

Key elements of a case study in the context of bidding for contracts include:

- Project Description: A description of the specific project or contract that was undertaken by the bidder, including its scope, objectives, and key deliverables.

- Client Information: Information about the client or organisation for whom the project was completed, including their industry, sector, and any relevant background information.

- Challenges and Solutions: Identification of any challenges, obstacles, or complexities encountered during the project, along with the strategies, solutions, and approaches employed to overcome them.

- Methodology and Approach: An explanation of the methodologies, techniques, and approaches used by the bidder to execute the project and achieve the desired outcomes.

- Results and Achievements: A summary of the results, achievements, and outcomes of the project, including measurable metrics, key performance indicators, and any notable successes or benefits realised by the client.

- Client Testimonials or References: Testimonials, feedback, or references from the client or stakeholders involved in the project, attesting to the bidder's performance, quality of work, and professionalism.

- Relevance to Current Bid: Demonstrating how the experience and lessons learned from the case study are relevant and applicable to the current bid or project being pursued.

Including case studies in a bid proposal helps to provide concrete evidence of the bidder's capabilities, credibility, and suitability for the contract being sought. By showcasing successful past projects and demonstrating the ability to deliver results, case studies can significantly strengthen the bidder's overall bid and increase their chances of winning the contract. So, a case study for RentaLorry might look something like the very simple example below:

Contract:	Weekly delivery of craft supplies to retailers	
Client:	Craftysuppliescostless Ltd	
Duration:	Jan 2023 to Dec 2024, ongoing	

Contract Value:	£100,000.00 GBP
Location:	UK wide

Overview of our contract delivery

RentaLorry were contracted by Craftysuppliescostless Ltd to undertake weekly delivery of supplies to retailers across the UK.

Careful planning of routes, aligned with convenient pick up and drop off times were enabled using our state of the art 'getitthereontime' automated software. This represented a saving to the client of circa £10,000 on previous identical contracts.

This contract required the mobilisation of 5 lorries and a core and pool team of 15 skilled and experienced, licensed drivers responding to very tight programmes.

"We were so delighted with RentaLorry being able to jump to and save the day, not to mention £'s in penalties. We would recommend them to any retailer as a delivery company of choice." Ted Theboss, Craftysuppliescostless Ltd.

Build a library of these and evidencing your capability will be really easy.

6. Social Value

You will need to build a library of evidence of social value. That is business activity that has benefitted your local community or charities.

Social value refers to the positive impact a business or organisation generates for the community, environment, and society as a whole beyond its core economic activities. It involves contributing to social well-being, environmental sustainability, and community development.

Evidencing social value is essential for demonstrating the broader positive effects of your business beyond financial metrics. Here are a few ways to evidence social value in your business:

Impact Assessment:

- Conduct a comprehensive impact assessment to identify and measure the social, environmental, and economic outcomes of your activities.
- Use key performance indicators (KPIs) that align with your business goals and social impact objectives.
- Stakeholder Engagement:
- Engage with stakeholders, including customers, employees, local communities, and suppliers, to understand their needs and expectations.
- Solicit feedback on the social value initiatives you've implemented.

Case Studies and Success Stories:

- Showcase specific examples or case studies illustrating how your business has positively impacted individuals or communities.
- Highlight success stories to provide tangible evidence of your commitment to social value.

Partnerships and Collaborations:

- Highlight partnerships with local charities, non-profits, or community organisations.
- Emphasize collaborative initiatives that have resulted in positive social outcomes.

Employment and Training:

- Demonstrate your commitment to fair employment practices, diversity, and inclusion.
- Provide evidence of training programs, apprenticeships, or initiatives that enhance the skills and employability of your workforce.

Environmental Practices:

- Showcase sustainable and environmentally friendly practices within your business operations.
- Provide evidence of initiatives that reduce your carbon footprint, waste, or resource consumption.

Community Investment:

-   Outline financial or in-kind contributions to community projects, events, or initiatives.
-   Detail how your business supports local economic development and community well-being.

Transparent Reporting:

-   Incorporate social value metrics and impact data into your regular reporting processes.
-   Publish transparent reports that detail your social, environmental, and economic performance.

Certifications and Standards:

-   Consider obtaining certifications or adhering to standards related to social responsibility, environmental sustainability, or ethical business practices.
-   Certifications like B Corp can provide third-party validation of your commitment to social value.

Social Return on Investment (SROI):

-   Utilise methodologies like Social Return on Investment (SROI) to quantitatively measure the social and environmental value generated by your business activities.

By combining quantitative data, qualitative stories, and engagement with stakeholders, you can effectively evidence the social value created by your business. This not only enhances your reputation but also demonstrates a commitment to making a positive impact beyond profit.

7. Environment and Sustainability

Critical to almost every bid is to be able to prove how your services, products and/or operations are environmentally friendly and sustainable. i.e., your strategy to achieve net zero, how you deal with waste etc.

This means that you will have to set a baseline, i.e., where is your business now in terms of environment and sustainability. Creating that baseline is a crucial step in measuring improvements in environment and sustainability targets for your business.

Here's what you need to do:

Identify Key Metrics:

-   Determine the key environmental and sustainability metrics relevant to your business. These could include energy consumption, waste generation, water usage, carbon emissions, and more.

Gather Historical Data:

-   Collect historical data for each identified metric. Look back over a specific period (e.g., the past year or several years) to understand your business's past performance.

Define Scope and Boundaries:

- Clearly define the scope and boundaries of your baseline assessment. Consider whether you'll assess the entire organisation or specific departments, locations, or processes.

Engage Stakeholders:

- Involve relevant stakeholders, including employees, suppliers, and customers, in the data collection process. Their insights can contribute to a more comprehensive understanding of your business's environmental impact.

Select a Reference Year or Period:

- Choose a reference year or period against which you'll measure future improvements. This will serve as the baseline against which progress will be assessed.

Use Standardised Measurement Units:

- Ensure that all metrics are measured using standardised units to facilitate accurate comparisons over time. For example, express energy consumption in kilowatt-hours (kWh) or carbon emissions in metric tons.

Consider External Factors:

- Account for external factors that may influence your business's environmental performance, such as changes in industry standards, regulations, or market conditions.

Calculate Intensity Metrics:

-   If applicable, calculate intensity metrics that normalise environmental performance against a specific output metric (e.g., energy consumption per unit of production).

Document Methodology:

-   Clearly document the methodology used for data collection and calculation. Transparency in your approach enhances the credibility of your baseline assessment.

Assess Data Quality:

-   Ensure the accuracy and reliability of your data. Regularly review and validate data sources to maintain data quality.

Benchmark Against Standards:

-   Benchmark your baseline against industry standards, if available, to gain insights into how your business compares with peers.

Communicate Results:

-   Communicate the baseline findings to internal and external stakeholders. This transparency fosters awareness and commitment to sustainability goals.

Set Targets and Goals:

-   Based on the baseline assessment, set realistic and measurable targets for improvement. These targets should align with your business's overall sustainability objectives.

Implement Monitoring Systems:

- Establish robust monitoring systems to track ongoing performance and gather data for future assessments.

Regularly Review and Update:

- Conduct regular reviews of your baseline, updating it as needed to reflect changes in your business, industry, or external factors.

By following these steps, you'll create a solid baseline that serves as a foundation for measuring and demonstrating improvements in your business's environmental and sustainability performance over time. Demonstrating the improvements you make is all evidence of your commitment to environment and sustainability that you can use in your bids.

8. Resources

Do you have the right people in place, and can you evidence their skills and qualifications in terms of the delivery of any contract you are bidding for? Thinking you can recruit IF you win will not be acceptable to potential clients.

At the very least make sure that you and your employees have up to date CVs on file at all times. Both full CVs and mini versions, as bids vary in what they require and you don't want to be developing a new mini-

CV for every bid for each employee.

Most bids will ask for some evidence of your capacity to deliver the contract in terms of the people you have available and their ability to perform the requirements to the required standard.

If you deliver multiple contracts you may need to also evidence that the resources specified for this contract are not committed to other contracts already. But I'm sure you have staff workflows and availability charts in place, right?

9. Know what's coming

Deciding to submit a bid only when the tender is released, without building relationships and doing research is risky. Making sure you have steps 1 to 8 in place, having created your library of evidence and built those relationships and sussed out the competition you just need to find those opportunities.

In plenty of time to develop and submit a bid. We will go into this later in the book to give you an idea of where to look.

10. Can you afford to invest?

Bidding is expensive. Use experts if you don't know how or you will be throwing your money and time away.

As you can see from points 1 to 9 there is a lot of work to do even before you start bidding but once that foundation is built (and kept up to date!) bidding becomes much easier, less time consuming and has a greater chance of success.

Even if you hire an external bid specialist there are savings to be made if you can supply the collateral, they need to craft the bid responses without them having to spend time doing it for you.

Remember bidding costs can be around 10% of the contract fee so shouldn't be rushed in to gung ho. Great preparation is key.

Only when you need us

So, unless you have the income to support a permanent in-house bid resource or team then outsourcing, as and when you need it, may be the wise interim measure.

Professional support to win work that grows your income to the levels needed to move everything in-house. Less risk, more opportunity.

Nobody does it better

To paraphrase Nanny McPhee:

'When you need us, but do not want us, we are there for you. When you want us, but no longer need us then we have done what we set out to do'.

In essence, as we work with you, we upskill you and build your collateral so that eventually you can do it by yourself. But we will still be there when you need cover for absence or just because you know that nobody does it better . . .

Keiths insight from the lonely seat

If I had just read this chapter for the first time, seen what is involved in making a successful bid, in honesty my first reaction would be to snap the book shut and hide it away somewhere never to be re-opened. The amount of work required seems daunting and hugely time consuming. But then when I took a step back, I can see that the long-term potential of putting in the work can be immense, not least because many if not most of my competitors won't bother. On the face of it the task seems daunting, but like all things, once we have learned what we need to learn, then the road opens up to the horizon.

If you think about it, the difference between run of the mill businesses and the ones who become high fliers is that the latter make these kinds of investments in time and resources.

In the past, I would have tried to take all of the steps outlined in this chapter myself.

Nowadays I am older and wiser, in the words of Dan Sullivan, the question is "who not how".

You are surrounded by staff who given the chance can interact and network with potential clients. (Your team will be all the better for it.) If you don't have the team to carry out all of the necessary work Ali has outlined in this chapter, then outsource it! Whether you choose to do so always has to be your choice but take two major factors into consideration when you make that choice.

- It's a decision which should be judged on long term benefits, not necessarily just a short-term marketing exercise.
- Whatever you do, make sure that everything is done up to a standard not down to a price.

Beach of Gold

Beach of Gold

CHAPTER 4: NAVIGATING THE WORLD OF CONTRACTS

Introduction

Navigating the World of Contracts when it comes to bidding for private and public sector contracts, for those of you who are new to this game, is like sailing around Cape Horn in a storm, in a blow-up dingy.

Now, you have to sail around it; contracts are unavoidable in business, and you won't find many more complex than those for tenders. But you can increase your chances of a smooth sailing with a little expert insight on what to look out for.

Brace yourself . . .

Understanding the Landscape

When you download the tender documents for any bid, you should see a copy of the contract that you will have to sign if you win.

If it's not there, Tip number 1 is to request a copy because there is no point in spending time and money on bidding if the terms of the contract are going to be unacceptable or unfulfillable for you.

Tip number 2 is to read that contract first, thoroughly, and note any questions you may have for the procurement team and get them in before the clarification deadline passes.

Identifying issues in the contract that may need attention

Below, you will see a list of typical contract contents that you need to understand in terms of their impact on you and your business if you win the contract. This is by no means a complete list, but it does cover some of the key areas you need to be aware of.

1. INTRODUCTION
2. DEFINITIONS AND INTERPRETATION
3. DURATION AND PURPOSE OF THE CONTRACT
4. PAYMENT OF FEES AND PAYMENT PROCEDURE
5. ELIGIBLE AND INELIGIBLE EXPENDITURE
6. CONTRACT REVIEW
7. MONITORING AND REPORTING
8. PROJECT EVALUATION, AUDITING AND ASSURANCE
9. FINANCIAL MANAGEMENT AND PREVENTION OF BRIBERY, CORRUPTION, FRAUD AND OTHER IRREGULARITY
10. CONFLICTS OF INTEREST
11. CONFIDENTIALITY
12. TRANSPARENCY
13. STATUTORY DUTIES
14. PUBLIC PROCUREMENT AND DATA PROTECTION
15. INTELLECTUAL PROPERTY RIGHTS
16. ENVIRONMENTAL REQUIREMENTS
17. ASSETS
18. INSURANCE

So, let's look at these in a little more detail.

1. INTRODUCTION

This is usually a statement of the parties involved, buyer and supplier, the value of the contract and a summary of 'the conditions'.

You may also see something like the following: 'The Parties confirm that it is their intention to be legally contractually bound by this Agreement.' So make sure you read through the whole document and are happy to be legally bound by its terms and conditions.

2. DEFINITIONS AND INTERPRETATION

This will be a list of terms and/or acronyms relating to the conditions of the contract to provide clarity of meaning. Usually in alphabetical order, make sure you understand all the entries in this section and raise questions where it is unclear or suggests onerous conditions that you are not happy with.

3. DURATION AND PURPOSE OF THE CONTRACT

The entries here are part of the conditions of the contract and may include dates and durations, milestones to be achieved, the process for making or requesting changes during the contract, activities or deadlines etc. Make sure that you are able to meet these conditions from the outset.

4. PAYMENT OF FEES AND PAYMENT PROCEDURE

This section will detail the limits of the fees payable, the process for payment and the conditions of payment.

Pay careful attention to the payment terms specified. For instance, you may only be able to claim payment quarterly in arrears, and there may be a 90-day payment period. This means that you might not get your first payment until 6 months after you commence the work. Can your business sustain this? As a rule, payments tend to be claimable 30 days in arrears with a 30-day payment period, but even that is 2 months.

This is a very important section and needs to be clearly understood and workable for your business.

5. ELIGIBLE AND INELIGIBLE EXPENDITURE

This section will detail what you can and can't invoice the supplier for. Check this carefully, as things like travel expenses, marketing and marketing materials, or required software may not be claimable and should be considered when pricing your tender response.

For certain, you will not be reimbursed for any costs relating to any element of developing and submitting your tender response.

6. CONTRACT REVIEW

This section should detail when and how your performance will be measured in terms of contract delivery. This may include elements of monitoring and reporting, which will be detailed in the following section.

It may include a specific software requirement for reporting, which may or may not be an allowable expense. Check eligible and ineligible expenditures.

7. MONITORING AND REPORTING

Monthly or quarterly reporting, meetings required, KPI deliverables, these should all be detailed here. Make sure that whatever the requirements are, that you can meet them.

For instance, if you are required to travel to face-to-face review meetings every month, what will that cost in terms of time and money, and do you have the resources for that if it is not covered in the contract eligible expenditure?

What resources do you need to collate and produce the necessary reporting, who needs to be at the meetings? All this may impact your delivery costs so needs to be weighed up and included in your financial proposal. This is tricky because so many bids have a high weighting on the financial submission so you need to be competitive. (knowing your competition is key here – see the Art of Capture Planning in Chapter 8)

8. PROJECT EVALUATION, AUDITING AND ASSURANCE

This section should outline how the client will measure your performance, your project/contract spend, the documents and records required to be kept ready for inspection (audit), and the access the client must have to carry out the audits it specifies.

Making sure that you have everything in place for this can be costly in terms of time and resources needed, and so, again, this needs to be considered in your pricing.

You want to win the contract, but it has to be profitable, right?

9. FINANCIAL MANAGEMENT AND PREVENTION OF BRIBERY, CORRUPTION, FRAUD AND OTHER IRREGULARITY

'The supplier will at all times comply with all applicable Laws, statutes and regulations relating to anti-bribery and anti-corruption, including but not limited to the Bribery Act.'

This statement normally also extends to any subcontractors you may engage in the delivery of the contract so all parties need to sign up to this.

You should also have a 'Prevention of Bribery, Corruption, Fraud and Other Irregularity Policy in place in your business. This may be asked for as part of your submission.

The penalties for any contravention of the laws surrounding Bribery, Corruption and Fraud may also be stated here.

10. CONFLICTS OF INTEREST

If you win the contract and it turns out your brother is on the procurement panel, then you will be in trouble. This is known as 'a conflict of interest'.

This section may cover what constitutes a conflict of interest for this contract and may require you to confirm, in a written statement, that there are no conflicts of interest. So make sure there aren't; otherwise, you open yourself up to a world of trouble!

11. CONFIDENTIALITY

Contracts are, by their nature, confidential documents, as are elements of or all of the activities in your delivery of a contract. What confidentiality means for the contract you are bidding for should be clearly stated in this section.

Make sure you are able to provide the confidentiality required.

12. TRANSPARENCY

This section should include something like this, 'The Parties acknowledge that, except for any information which is exempt from disclosure in accordance with the provisions of the Information Acts, the content of the Agreement is not confidential.'

So be sure what is exempt from disclosure and what isn't.

For a contract section entitled 'Transparency', very often, what is stated is about as clear as mud!!

13. STATUTORY DUTIES

The conditions of the contract that are governed by law should be listed here. These might include compliance with specific acts or legislation. Adherence to specific data protection laws may be stated, and advice on specific documents you may need to be able to submit during the contract might be given here.

Having a data protection policy in place for your business is useful as this might be asked for as part of your bid submission.

14. PUBLIC PROCUREMENT AND DATA PROTECTION

Often found in public sector contracts, this section will detail the requirements of the supplier (you) in terms of acceptance of alignment with the policies and procedures of the buyer (the client) and their procurement regulations.

This section will also outline the procedures in place to ensure data protection, such as storage and transfer protocols.

Again, watch out for a specific software requirement, and if one is stated, make sure that it is an allowable expense to purchase and/or install it.

15. INTELLECTUAL PROPERTY RIGHTS

Be very careful here. Watch out for statements in this section that suggest, blatantly or subtly, that any ideas, processes, products, or inventions will belong to the buyer. You may be developing a product that you might lose all rights to. That may be acceptable; just be sure you know what your rights are here.

I once worked with an infrastructure client who had developed a traffic modelling system for a client. The contract stated that all intellectual property developed during the contract would remain in the possession of the client. The supplier ended up paying for a license to the client, for a system they had developed. We were very careful when assessing IP rights for the contract I worked with them on.

16. ENVIRONMENTAL REQUIREMENTS

The client may put targets here relating to emissions, waste reduction, use of water, etc. in relation to your contract delivery. Ensure these are understood and that you can meet those targets.

Pay special attention to any penalties payable for failure to meet targets specified.

Also, if this kind of clause is in the contract, then it might be an idea to ensure that your proposal details how you will meet those specific targets, why that is important to you and how your approach to environment and sustainability aligns with theirs. (Know your client – the Art of Capture Planning in Chapter 8)

17. ASSETS

This section should outline what belongs to whom in terms of assets specific to this contract. It may also state the value of assets below which no reporting is necessary. It may also outline the requirement for the disposal of any assets created or acquired during the contract period.

Make sure you get clarity on this otherwise you may lose out or end up in disputes about ownership, particularly where assets have been purchased and paid for as an eligible expense.

18. INSURANCE

You will need to have certain insurances in place. This section should specify which insurances and the minimum level of cover that should be in place for the delivery of this contract. They will want to see copies of your certification for all required insurances either as part of your bid submission or upon commencement of the contract.

19. ASSIGNMENT

This is about transferring activities, monies or assets associated with this contract to third parties such as subcontractors. Any assignment will usually require written permission from the client prior to transfer.

20. FORCE MAJEURE

Force Majeure (unforeseeable circumstances that prevent someone from fulfilling a contract) should be specified in any contract as 'Neither Party shall be in breach of this Agreement by reason of any Force Majeure Event.' And usually, each party will be required to bear their own costs arising as a consequence of any Force Majeure Event.

Examples of Force Majeure events are war, strike, riot, crime, epidemic, or sudden legal change that prevents one or both parties from fulfilling their obligations under the contract.

Explicitly excluded is any event described as an 'Act of God', which covers a separate domain and legally differs, though it is related to contract law.

An Act of God is an event outside of human control or activity. Here are some examples of Acts of God:

- Floods
- Tornadoes
- Lightning
- Hailstorms
- Earthquakes
- Fires (if caused by lightning or another natural force)
- Volcanic eruptions

21. SPENDING CONTROLS – MARKETING, ADVERTISING, COMMUNICATIONS AND CONSULTANCY

This section should detail which party is responsible for which activities and costs in relation to any spending required by the contract.

Be very clear on this because some expenses, like marketing or consultancy, can be cost prohibitive; if the responsibility is yours, you need to consider this before you start preparing your bid.

22. LOSSES, GIFTS AND SPECIAL PAYMENTS

This section usually details what permissions are needed from the client before actions, including losses, gifts and special payments are incurred. It can also include spending limits or other restrictions.

23. BORROWING

This may outline any exclusions where you, as a supplier, might be thinking about borrowing monies to deliver the contract (often as a result of difficult payment terms specified in the contract), so make sure you understand this as guarantees of financial solvency may be required.

24. PUBLICITY

What you can and can't publicise about your work on the contract should be detailed here.

There may be restrictions due to IP or confidentiality issues and these should be stated and agreed to.

The methodology of creating publicity, such as restrictions on the use of social media may be stated here. Be careful not to break the rules as penalties may be enforced for non-compliance.

25. CHANGES TO THE STATUTORY REQUIREMENTS

It may be that the contract is funded, or part funded by government or another statutory body. This section should detail what will happen if that body makes changes that affect the delivery or funding of the contract and its impact on all parties.

26. CLAWBACK, EVENTS OF DEFAULT, TERMINATION AND RIGHTS RESERVED FOR BREACH AND TERMINATION

It is very important to be clear on the elements included in this section. It should outline fees and penalties payable for missed deadlines, poor performance, and other activities that may be considered unacceptable by the client.

Think about what impact the conditions in this section might have on your business if you fail to deliver as promised.

27. DISPUTE RESOLUTION

Most contracts include a measure of trust and good faith from all parties; however, sometimes things go wrong, and there may be disputes about blame, recompense or other elements of the contract.

This section should detail how disputes will be managed, whether there is any prevention of either side commencing legal proceedings and what any escalation process might entail.

Be very clear on this one. Remember this contract will be legally binding and so you must understand the risks associated with any dispute.

28. LIMITATION OF LIABILITY

Usually, this section states that the client accepts no responsibility for anything that goes wrong, directly or indirectly.

It may also state that you, the supplier, must indemnify and hold harmless any stakeholder, funding body or the client in respect to any actions, claims, charges or demands arising from the contract.

It is crucial that you understand and accept any limitation of liability before you proceed to bid.

29. VAT

This will simply be a statement of the client's policy in terms of the payment of VAT in relation to the contract payments.

30. CODE OF CONDUCT

If the client's code of conduct is not included in the tender documents, then request a copy of this clause in the contract because you will be deemed as accepting all of the principles included in it upon signing of the contract.

You may even be asked to submit a signed agreement accepting the principles of the Code of Conduct with your bid documents.

31. NOTICES

This is about the process/rules concerning notices and communications and may look something like this:

All notices and other communications in relation to this Agreement shall be in writing and shall be deemed to have been duly given if personally delivered, e-mailed, or mailed (first class postage prepaid) to the address of the relevant party, as referred to in Schedule xxx or otherwise notified in writing. All notices and other communications must be marked for the attention of the contact specified in Schedule xxx (Contact Details). If personally delivered or if e-mailed, all such communications shall be deemed to have been given when received (except that if received on a non-working day or after 5.00 pm on any Working Day, they shall be deemed received on the next Working Day), and if mailed all such communications shall be deemed to have been given and received on the second Working Day following such mailing.

Just check that you are okay with this process and work it into your delivery plan.

32. GOVERNING LAW

This is a statement of legal compliance with the contract. For contracts issued in England it might read as: 'These Conditions will be governed by and construed in accordance with the law of England and the Parties irrevocably submit to the exclusive jurisdiction of the English courts.'

———

There are, of course, limitless clauses and conditions in contracts and to cover them all here isn't possible, so we have just picked a few to start getting you familiar with what to look out for.

Our best advice is to get a contract law specialist to review it if you have any questions.

Keith's insight from the Lonely Seat

German-born architect Ludwig Mies van der Rohe (1886-1969) has been credited with the idiom "The Devil is in the detail", although chances are that he lifted it from an earlier German phrase which translated as "God is in the detail". In terms of what Ali has discussed here, the reference to the Devil being in the detail is more apt. On the subject of quotations and idioms, one coined by William Congreve in the late 17th century is even more appropriate in this context ... "Marry in haste, we may repent at leisure". Whether you use outside help or do everything in-house, don't cut corners. How often, over the years, are we caught out by "small print"?

But it's not all doom and gloom; all of this detail, all of this having to satisfy what seem to be the most banal conditions, means that few will venture beyond page one. With the right help, it can be dealt with relatively easily. If business was easy, everyone would have one, right? It's a chance to put ourselves ahead of the competition.

Beach of Gold

CHAPTER 5: DECODING TENDERS

Introduction

If you think contracts are tricky, try dissecting an Invitation to Tender document and the accompanying specification! Of course, this book has been written specifically to help you navigate this minefield safely, and in this chapter, we show you how.

The Tender Documents

When you register/express interest in a bid opportunity, you will be able to access a number of bid documents. This may be via a tendering portal or, although less likely, by requesting the documents via email or post.

Here are the main documents you can expect the client to issue, starting with the four core documents you will nearly always see:

Invitation to Tender (ITT) or Request for Proposal (RFP): This is the formal document that invites potential suppliers to submit a bid for the engineering project. It outlines the project details, requirements, and the process for submitting a proposal.

Instructions to Bidders: This document provides guidance on how suppliers should prepare and submit their bids. It may include information on the format, structure, and deadline for submitting proposals, as well as any specific requirements for the bid.

Scope of Work or Technical Specifications: This outlines the details of the engineering project, including the scope of work, technical requirements, and any specific standards or specifications that must be met. It helps suppliers understand the technical aspects of the project.

Contract Terms and Conditions: This document outlines the legal and contractual terms and conditions that will govern the relationship between the buyer and the successful bidder. It includes details such as payment terms, delivery schedules, warranties, and other contractual obligations.

You may also receive:

Evaluation Criteria: The criteria by which the procurement team will assess and compare the bids. This may include factors such as technical competence, price, experience, and compliance with specifications.

Bid Form: This is the template or form that suppliers use to submit their bids. It typically includes sections for pricing, technical details, and any other information required by the procurement team.

Qualification Criteria: The minimum requirements that suppliers must meet to be eligible to bid. This may include financial stability, relevant experience, and technical capabilities.

Submission Timetable: Clearly defined dates and times for the submission of bids. Late submissions may not be considered.

Contact Information: Details of whom to contact for clarification or additional information related to the bidding process.

TUPE: Transfer of Undertakings (Protection of Employment) Regulations information (TUPE)

These documents collectively provide a comprehensive overview of the project and the requirements for potential suppliers to prepare and submit their bids. It's important for both the procurement team and potential suppliers to adhere to the guidelines outlined in the tender documentation to ensure a fair and transparent bidding process.

The Specification (Scope of Works) in more detail

This is key to the tender; it outlines exactly what the buyer is looking for and what it wants to achieve, and every part of your response needs to relate back to this document and what it states.

A Specification document or "Scope of Work" (SOW) will be issued as part of a tender process and provides a detailed description of the tasks, responsibilities, deliverables, and specifications associated with a particular project. The purpose of the SOW is to communicate to potential suppliers exactly what is expected in terms of the work to be performed. The specific content of a Scope of Work can vary depending on the nature of the project, but it typically includes the following:

Project Overview: A brief description of the project, its objectives, and the context within which it will be executed.

Objectives and Deliverables: Clearly defined project objectives and the specific deliverables expected from the supplier upon completion of the project.

Scope Boundaries: Clear delineation of what is within the scope of the project and what is not. This helps avoid misunderstandings and scope creep.

Project Schedule: A timeline or schedule outlining key milestones, deadlines, and any critical dates related to the project.

Technical Specifications: Detailed technical requirements, standards, and specifications that must be adhered to in the execution of the work.

Qualitative Requirements: Any qualitative criteria or expectations for the work, such as quality standards, performance criteria, or industry best practices.

Roles and Responsibilities: A breakdown of the roles and responsibilities of the supplier and, if applicable, the buyer's team. This includes information on project management, communication, and reporting structures.

Site Conditions (if applicable): Information about the physical conditions or constraints at the project site that may impact the execution of the work.

Regulatory and Compliance Requirements: Any legal or regulatory requirements that the supplier must adhere to during the course of the project.

Health and Safety Requirements: Details regarding health and safety standards that must be followed to ensure a safe working environment.

Insurance and Liability: Requirements: for insurance coverage and any liabilities associated with the project.

Payment Terms: Details about how and when payments will be made to the supplier, including any milestones or payment schedules.

Performance Metrics: Specific metrics or key performance indicators (KPIs) by which the success of the project will be measured.

Contractual Terms and Conditions: Reference to the overarching contract terms and conditions that govern the relationship between the buyer and the supplier.

A well-drafted Scope of Work is crucial for both the buyer and potential suppliers, as it provides a clear understanding of project expectations, minimises misunderstandings, and facilitates the evaluation of bids during the tender process.

It is essential that you read and dissect this document and raise any queries with the client before the cut-off date for such queries passes.

Building a Successful Bid

Read all of the documents issued by the procurement team. Let me say that again: Read all of the documents issued by the procurement team. More importantly, understand exactly what they are asking for and craft your proposal to address that.

Once you have done that, and believe me that takes time and patience, then and only then do you begin to build your response.

There are, more often than not, specific templates into which you need to insert your bid responses. These may be fields you type directly into on the portal (I suggest you write it offline first, then copy and paste your final version!), or they may be Word templates you download and fill in, ready to be uploaded as final documents.

Either way, make sure you understand the requirements and formats (read the instructions for bidders) before you start. Note that there will probably be word/page count restrictions and instructions regarding font size, layout, graphics, etc.

The specific documents that are required to be completed and returned to procurement for assessment may vary depending on the procurement process and the instructions provided in the tender documentation. However, some key documents typically need to be completed and returned as part of the bid submission. These commonly include:

Bid Form: This is a critical document that suppliers must complete to provide pricing details, technical specifications, and any other information required by the buyer. The bid form often serves as a structured template for suppliers to present their bids in a standardised manner.

Qualification Criteria: Suppliers may need to submit documentation proving they meet the minimum qualification criteria outlined in the tender documentation. This could include financial statements, proof of relevant experience, certifications, or other evidence of their capabilities. This may take the form of a Selection Questionnaire or just be a number of questions in the bid form template.

Documentation Supporting Technical Proposal: If the tender requires a detailed technical proposal, suppliers must complete and submit documentation supporting their proposed approach to the project. This may include project plans, methodologies, and other technical details.

Compliance Statement: A document affirming that the bidder agrees to comply with all the terms and conditions outlined in the tender documentation, including the scope of work, contractual terms, and other requirements.

Proof of Insurance and Liability Coverage: If specified in the tender documentation, suppliers may need to provide proof of insurance coverage and details of their liability coverage.

Signed Contract Terms and Conditions: Suppliers typically need to acknowledge their acceptance of the contract terms and conditions by signing and returning the relevant documents. This includes agreeing to the terms of payment, delivery schedules, and other contractual obligations.

Any Other Specific Requirements: Depending on the nature of the project, there may be additional documents or information that the procurement team requires for assessment. These could include environmental impact assessments, safety plans, CVs, organisation charts or other project-specific documents.

It's crucial for suppliers to carefully review the tender documentation and follow the instructions provided by the procurement team. Failure to complete and return the required documents may result in the bid being deemed non-compliant or incomplete, potentially leading to disqualification from the procurement process. Therefore, attention to detail and adherence to the submission requirements are essential for a successful bid.

Creating a pack for the bid, which includes a Summary of Key Points to inform the writers and reviewers, is a useful undertaking at the start of the process. It also works as an agenda for a start-up meeting. This should include, as a minimum:

- Name of the Opportunity
- Purchasing Client
- Link to the Portal (including password and user name for those who need access only)
- Links to a shared folder containing the tender documents, Work in Progress Folder etc.
- Contract value, duration and location
- Bid lead name and contact details
- The bid timetable

- Overview of requirements: A summary of the specifications issued by the client
- A list of the Quality Questions to be responded to
- Questions the review team need to address.
- The bid programme including deadlines, review dates, submission dates etc. and who is responsible for each activity.
- Win themes identified / essential client intel and hot buttons
- Bid Document Format Instructions: including font type and size, margins, document naming conventions, word/page counts for each question
- Graphics / Chart requirements/restrictions, CV Requirements/restrictions
- Stakeholders

Keith's insight from the Lonely Seat

Once again, all of these conditions and compliance boxes that need to be ticked look pretty daunting. But how do you eat an elephant? The answer is, of course, one bite at a time. If you take on too much, all that you'll be left with is a severe case of indigestion.

If we dissect all of what's needed into bite-size chunks, then the prospect of completing a bid successfully and to a level required to stand a chance of winning becomes far less daunting. And having gone through the exercise the first time, the process becomes steadily easier.

This is a great opportunity to create a team spirit by delegating different aspects to others, giving them the responsibility to bring what they have produced to the rest of the team. It should go without saying that we can't simply foist that responsibility onto someone, they have to embrace it. But the difference it can make to their whole work ethic can be profound. Once again, the complexity of the overall task, when split into its component parts is not nearly so daunting. Yet those staff members who have embraced the challenge of creating a response to even just one of those parts will feel justifiably proud that they have been part of the whole complex bid.

One more thing...It's kind of a word of warning. I know that Ali has touched on this already, but it bears repeating. It's too easy to get too close to the work we carry out in complex matters such as this. One person reviewing their own work before submission is a recipe for disaster. Unseen faults and errors will almost certainly slip through. Better to create a framework where every contributor understands what's needed and helps check other contributors' work. That way it becomes an overtly team effort.

If you win, then you will have won together, but if you lose, then you might find that losing together brings your team even closer.

Beach of Gold

CHAPTER 6: TEAM MANAGEMENT ESSENTIALS

Introduction

Unless you are a one-man/woman band with no team or external support, you will be developing your bids on your own. You are your team, and we sincerely hope that this book will help you in that endeavour.

In this chapter, for those of you that do have a team, partners, external resources, we explore the pivotal components of forming and guiding that bid team, focusing on delegation, selecting the right individuals with the appropriate skills, and fostering a collaborative environment conducive to achieving bid excellence.

Assembling and Leading Winning Teams

You may be the boss, you may think you know more than anyone else about what you do, and so you might think that you are the natural person to lead the bid team. In actual fact this might not be the case.

In the competitive landscape of procurement, assembling and leading a winning bid team, particularly in a Small to Medium-sized Enterprise (SME) environment, demands strategic foresight, adept leadership, and a meticulous approach to team composition.

The Art of Delegation

Effective delegation lies at the heart of bid leadership. Recognising the strengths and capabilities of team members while understanding the intricate demands of each bid is fundamental. Delegation is not merely about assigning tasks; it's about entrusting responsibilities to individuals who possess the requisite expertise and empowering them to excel in their roles. This may well include appointing someone other than the boss as team lead.

Here are a few things to consider when delegating tasks within a bid team:

Clarity of Objectives: Clearly articulate the objectives, scope, and expectations of the bid project to ensure alignment among team members.

Match Tasks to Skills: Assign tasks based on individual strengths, competencies, and experience, ensuring each team member contributes meaningfully to the bid process.

Empowerment through Authority: Provide team members with the authority and autonomy necessary to make informed decisions within their designated areas of responsibility.

Establish Accountability: Support a culture of accountability in which team members take ownership of their tasks and deliverables, promoting a sense of collective responsibility for bid success.

Selecting the Right Individuals

In the dynamic landscape of bid management, selecting the right individuals for the team is paramount. Beyond technical prowess, the ideal bid team should comprise individuals with diverse skills, experiences, and perspectives, driving innovation and adaptability in navigating complex bidding scenarios.

Key considerations in selecting bid team members:

Technical Proficiency: Identify individuals with a robust understanding of bid management processes, including proposal writing, cost estimation, risk assessment, and compliance standards.

Interpersonal Skills: Prioritise candidates who demonstrate strong communication, collaboration, and negotiation skills, essential for cohesive team dynamics and client engagement.

Strategic Thinkers: Seek team members capable of strategic thinking and problem-solving, adept at navigating challenges and seizing opportunities throughout the bid lifecycle.

Resilience and Adaptability: Look for individuals who exhibit resilience and adaptability in the face of adversity, capable of thriving in high-pressure environments and driving continuous improvement.

Strategies for Efficient Collaboration

Successful bid teams thrive on a culture of collaboration, trust, and mutual respect. In any setting, supportive cohesion among team members is instrumental in maximising productivity, harnessing collective expertise, and delivering compelling bid submissions that resonate with clients.

Strategies for fostering collaboration within bid teams include:

Clear Communication Channels: Establish open lines of communication, leveraging both formal and informal channels to facilitate transparent dialogue, share insights, and address concerns effectively.

Team Building Activities: Encourage knowledge-sharing to foster camaraderie, strengthen interpersonal bonds, and enhance collective problem-solving capabilities.

Encourage Innovation: Cultivate an environment that encourages innovation and out-of-the-box thinking, empowering team members to explore creative solutions and challenge conventional approaches.

Celebrate Achievements: Recognise and celebrate individual and team achievements, reinforcing a culture of appreciation, motivation, and shared success.

In conclusion, assembling and leading winning bid teams in an SME environment requires a strategic blend of delegation, talent selection, and collaborative leadership. By empowering individuals, fostering a culture of excellence, and nurturing cohesive teamwork, SMEs can position themselves as formidable contenders in the competitive landscape of bid management, driving sustainable growth and client satisfaction.

Keith's insight from the Lonely Seat

I've been banging on about the importance and value of team building for years. What Ali has written in this chapter distils the thousands of words I've written into just a few hundred, yet she has in no way lost the importance. There is not much left for me to add here...well, maybe just a little.

Quite rightly, Ali speaks of giving people responsibility to deliver and ensuring they accept that responsibility and take ownership of the project. What I would add is that you shouldn't forget to look in the dark corners. Don't just cast your net over people who are in and out of your office every day.

If your business is of a certain size there will be people whose potential has been going unnoticed. Give them a chance. Yes, you might have to help them a little more than you would otherwise, but the rewards for the business if they succeed are off the scale. Not only will you have created a new productive and valuable asset, but in giving someone a chance to shine, you will have created a new ambassador for your business.

Beach of Gold

CHAPTER 7: LEARNING FROM THE PAST

Ok, I know this maybe should have come first in the book. I thought about it a lot. But in the end, my conclusion was that you first needed to understand what you were letting yourself in for before the practicalities of planning for it. I hope that makes sense.

Introduction

In the world of bidding, learning from the past is a fabulous way to grow in the future. Loosely speaking, this process is referred to as 'Lessons Learned' and feeds into 'Capture Planning'. We will look at both of these in this chapter.

Analysing Results for Continuous Improvement

This begins with the team's analysis of how it went, what could be done better next time, what went well, and the lessons learned from that, plus what to capture as evidence to use next time.

Ensure that after every bid submission, ideally before you get theresult, you hold a Lessons Learned Review with your bid team.

Once you have the result, there are two more activities, which will help you to capture information to help you do a better job next time. The first is a post-results lessons learned exercise, looking at the scoring and any feedback given by the procurement team. If they don't provide you with feedback, ask for it.

The second, which applies only when you have won a bid, is to continually gather client and end-user feedback throughout the delivery of the contract to use to make the next bid better than the last. This feeds into Capture Planning.

The Basics of Capture Planning

Now, maybe this should have come earlier in the book. Logically speaking, this is the pre-bid phase; before you bid, however, as you have the choice to read this book in any order you want, and as capture planning involves a fair bit of input and info from contracts previously won, we have put it here.

An Overview of the Capture Planning Process

On the following page you can see a basic overview of the capture planning process broken down into 3 core stages:

1. Research, Analyse & Validate
2. Develop & Outline
3. Influence Customer

All further structured into Activity, Focus and Capture Plan Elements

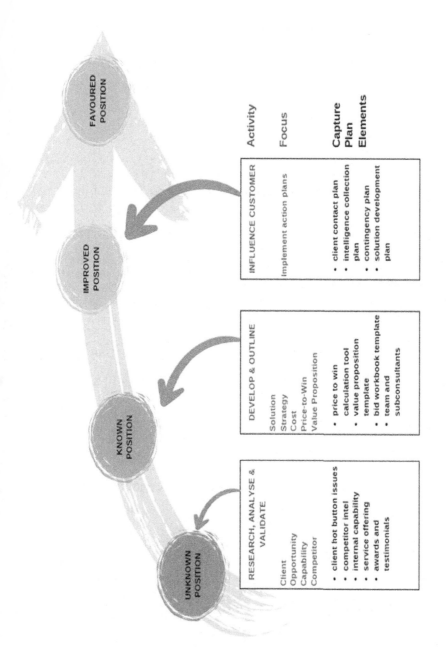

an overview of the Capture Planning Process

Capture Planning takes you from being an unknown entity with the client (Cold) through to being known, liked and trusted (Warm) and even, in some cases, invited to collaborate on developing the tender documents (Utopia).

The ten stages of capture planning are as follows:

1. Cold: Cold start, no existing relationship or pre-knowledge of the opportunity.

2. Scoping: Scoping, planning & intelligence gathering. Developing understanding and identifying gaps. We know our position, our competitors and our offer.

3. Key Client Management (KCM): Client or opportunity is from a key account. Direct invitation to bid. We know the decision-making unit.

4. Strategy: Capture strategy and focus developed and agreed. Early offer and your differentiators identified.

5. Engage: Engagement strategy underway, offer developing/developed and perceptions adjusting/adjusted.

6. Improve: Strengthen position and offer based on client feedback and information gained. Positive responses should be captured from any client relationship-building activity (networking, other services, etc.)

7. Test: Develop a two-way dialogue with prospective or existing clients around service requirements, improvements needed, and problems that need to be solved.

8. Top 3: Discussions with the client around the specification and procurement. Improvements can still be made.

9. Influence: Making final adjustments to the offer, relationships and profile to position yourself as a favourable bidder with a desirable offer.

10. Positioned to Win: You are positioned to win this work (60%+ likelihood of winning). (Utopia)

A good Capture Planning Strategy will:

- improve client relationships
- neutralise competitors
- protect/maintain relationships
- strengthen offer
- minimise risk
- qualify
- raise profile
- develop people
- improve track record

But if you don't take action in any of these areas to capture, share and analyse, then your position will never change. And trust me, your competition will be fierce, so you need to keep up.

Where does Capture Planning fit in your bid strategy?

As I am sure you are aware, as a business owner or CEO, you need a growth strategy. Capture planning and bidding sit within that overarching strategy.

Pictorially, it can be demonstrated like this:

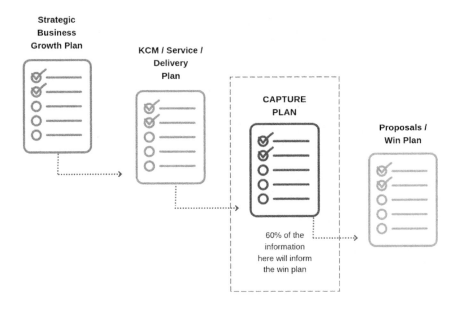

Now, where does capture planning sit in your overall bidding process? Well, again, it's best demonstrated graphically so on the following page is a typical bid process graphic. Be warned, it's multi=faceted but not as complex as it looks!

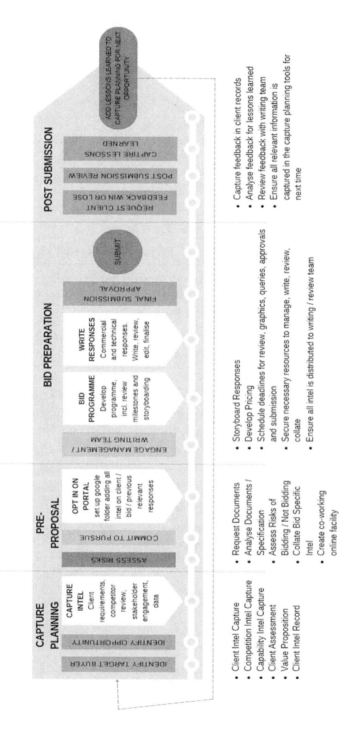

The Art of Capture Planning

This section will take you through capture planning in a little more detail. Step one is all about 'the 3 Cs' Client, Competition and Capability.

For each of these we need to look at what we know, identify what we don't know, and then fill those knowledge gaps.

CLIENT

What We May Know	What We May Not Know
List client drivers and issues we know (Hot Buttons)	What are the client's likely requirements & issues, motivators & hot buttons?
What do we know about their scope? Requirements?	Budgets & process – where is the funding coming from and how secure is it?
What is the problem they need to solve?	
What relationships do we have with the client's people?	Evaluators and influencers – who do we know, and what do they think of us? When did we last see them? How did we perform?
What is their budget?	
What is the background to their opportunity?	How strong is our organisational relationship? How does the client perceive us?
What are the risks of the project to the client?	What is our current position ... and what do we want it to be?

COMPETITION

What We May Know	What We May Not Know
List each of your competitors. Identify the strengths and weaknesses of each competitor: people/experience/ capability / their relationships with the client / their USPs / their approach. Rank all of these elements from weak, through level, to hard to beat.	Who are your competitors? How well are they thought of by the client? (they are only as good as their last job) What are their strengths? What are their weaknesses? What is their capability? Is their track record relevant? What innovations could they be selling? What is their availability? Do they have other distractions? Who else might they partner with?

CAPABILITY

What We May Know	What We May Not Know
What are your strengths and weaknesses? Can you offer a solution to the client's problem, to time and budget? What are the strengths and weaknesses of: Your team, resources, solutions, partners, experience, evidence. What is your USP?	Our options & outline of our best potential offer. Our best team (including partners and/ or stakeholders). Our experience. How we are perceived by the client. Our strengths and weaknesses. £££ How do we stack up?

Once you have looked at all this and captured useful information and insights, then you can begin to close any gaps:

Gap to Address	Ideas to Address it	How Long it Takes
Relationship	• Meet, introduce, face to face • Target individuals with individuals • Networking opportunities	6 months +
Organisational profile / perception	• Seminars • White papers • Conferences • Introduce others • Press • Ambassador	6 months +
Capability	• Explore internal capabilities • Opportunities for partnering to strengthen offer	3 months +
Capacity	• Opportunities for partnering to strengthen offer	3 months +
Experience	• Explore internal experience • Opportunities for partnering to strengthen offer	3 months +
Expertise	• Partnering • Recruitment • Upskill existing staff	3–6 months +
Innovations / Trends	• Guiding minds and thought leaders • Innovation workshops • Realisation • Proof / Evidence i.e. social value • Press	3 months +

A few more ideas to get you further towards that Utopia state as a bidder:

Keith's insight from the Lonely Seat

I know I have been making much of the bid writing/tendering process as an opportunity to grow a close-knit and thoroughly engaged team within a business, but in this chapter, another opportunity rings out loud and clear, like a church bell in a mountain valley.

To view one bid in isolation, with all the costs, trials and tribulations involved, is a mistake. Better to treat it as a learning process, a foundation upon which to build the next bid and the next one. The overall chance of winning will rise, and the costs of bidding will dramatically fall.

But the big win to be had here, and I mean the BIG WIN, if we are going to stand a reasonable chance of winning bids and growing our business is the opportunity to ask questions of our would-be clients.

Those questions are the opportunity to establish a relationship, and (unlike the usual banal sales questions) because they are likely to be seen by the client as us trying to do the best we possibly can for them, we go up in their estimation and start on the road to being perceived as a valuable supplier that can make their life easier.

And that puts us in the pound seats...ahead of the competition who will be treating the opportunity with far less respect.

There's nothing cynical about this, it's just a case of being seen to be caring and wanting to do the best job we can.

Beach of Gold

Beach of Gold

CHAPTER 8: CRAFTING WINNING RESPONSES

Introduction

We have already looked at bid documentation, and the plethora of forms and information you need to read and understand as well as complete and submit. This chapter dives a little deeper into the actual crafting of your responses.

The Anatomy of a Successful Bid

A successful bid will:

- Speak directly to the problem the client needs to solve. It's not about what you can do; it's about how what you do will benefit them, described, applied and evidenced
- Will be completely compliant with all of the requirements set out in the bid documentation
- Is concise and informative, no waffle.
- Is easy to read, signposting where necessary and totally relevant to the specification
- Actually answers the questions being asked

Best Practices for Response Creation

The basics of creating great responses to tender questions are as follows, and we will look at each one in more detail in the following pages:

1. Understand the question. Read it, analyse it, relate it to the specification and the problem needing to be solved.
2. Know precisely what that problem is and ensure everything you put in your response relates directly back to that problem. Not what you do, but how you do it and the benefits of that to the client.
3. Relate to the specification. If what you are writing has not been included in, alluded to or asked for in the specification, then it's probably not needed.
4. BARBIE: A methodology for great response writing
5. Make it interesting to read; the evaluator might have already read ten responses before yours, so you need to engage them.
6. Keep it in the word/ page count, text size, font type and check that words in charts and graphics will not be included in that count.
7. Keep your response succinct and relevant. To the point, and on point.

All of these practices come together in what we call The Storyboard.

The Storyboard

Creating a storyboard for a quality question in a bid is an effective way to organise your response and present information in a clear and structured manner. It is essential that the writer has read the specification and other relevant documents before developing any quality response. Here's a guide on what you might need to include in a storyboard for a quality question in a bid:

- Introduction: Provide a brief introduction to the technical question. Clearly state the problem or requirement you are addressing.
- Context and Background: Provide context to the technical question. Include any relevant background information that helps the evaluator understand the significance of the question.
- Objective: Clearly state the objective or goal of your response. Define what you aim to achieve in addressing the technical question.
- Methodology: Outline the approach or methodology you will use to answer the technical question. Break down the steps or stages involved in your approach.
- Technical Details: Present the technical details relevant to the question. Use diagrams, charts, or graphs to illustrate complex concepts. Include relevant data, calculations, or specifications.
- Risk Mitigation: Address any potential risks associated with your approach. Explain how you plan to mitigate these risks.
- Innovation or Value Proposition: Highlight any innovative aspects of your solution. Clearly articulate the value your solution brings to the project.
- Timeline: Provide a visual timeline or schedule for the implementation of your solution. Break down the project into phases or milestones.
- Resources: Specify the resources required to implement your

solution (e.g., personnel, equipment, materials). Include a breakdown of costs if applicable.

- Quality Assurance and Testing: Explain how you will ensure the quality of your solution. Detail any testing processes or quality control measures.
- Compliance and Standards: Demonstrate how your solution complies with relevant industry standards or regulations. Highlight any certifications or qualifications that support your approach.
- Conclusion: Summarise the key points of your response. Reiterate how your solution effectively addresses the technical question.
- Appendix: Include any additional supporting documents, technical specifications, or references. Attach relevant visuals, such as photographs, charts, or diagrams.

Each section should flow logically, providing a comprehensive, relevant and persuasive response to the technical question posed in the bid.

A typical Storyboard template can be found in the appendices to this book.

BARBie

Background / Action / Result / Benefit – is essential

This simple methodology may help you to create those complete and concise responses that win you bids.

Background: Begin each response, even each paragraph with background. Your understanding of the question, especially as it relates to the specification. An example of when you have solved this problem before. An example of your understanding of the problem the client needs to solve in relation to this question.

Action: Demonstrate the action you will take to solve the client's problem. Show how your service or product is ideally suited to solving the problem by explaining how it will operate as part of this contract. Show how taking this action previously has worked for others (testimonials / case studies). Show statistical information around the success of your actions.

Result: Talk about the results that the client will get from the actions you have outlined to solve their problem. Be as specific and detailed in terms of proof and statistical information as you can be. Demonstrate exactly the results you will deliver on this contract. A result is what will happen directly because of your actions.

Benefit: Benefits are different to results. Benefits are what will happen for the client because you have solved their problem. Talk about the benefits the clients will see because of the results of your solutions provision. i.e., raised turnover, more sleep, better staff retention, etc. Relate these benefits directly to the client's challenges and issues that have resulted in the need to contract for this work.

Follow this methodology as you develop your response and you will create great answers to the questions.

Do you fancy having a go at a very simple bid question? If so, here is the question, the specification and the compliance requirements.

The Question

Outline your methodology for the successful and cost-effective delivery of sandwiches to the Kindridge offices for the lifetime of the contract.

The Specification

The client (Kindridge) requires daily delivery of sandwiches to its offices in Telford between the hours of 11 am and noon.

The client will send the successful bidder its sandwich order before 9 am on each day that the service is required.

The successful bidder must ensure that there are sufficient choices for staff each day and that any changes to the core offering are communicated to the Kindridge contact person before 8 am.

Prices must be agreed upon before the commencement of this contract and may only be changed at intervals agreed between Kindridge and the client at the beginning of any business quarter.

This contract will commence on 1st April 2024 and end on 31st March 2025, subject to a one-year extension.

The Compliance Requirements

Your response must be submitted using the template on the next page.

Responses are limited to a word count of 200 words max, including words in graphics, diagrams, headings and tables. Font size must be Arial point 11.

Your response must be submitted to the client within 30 minutes of receiving the tender question.

No clarification questions are permitted.

Your response:

Q1: Outline your methodology for the successful and cost-effective delivery of sandwiches to the Kindridge offices for the lifetime of the contract.

Once you have written your response, go back and evaluate it against the question, the specification and the compliance. Is everything on point, to the point and BARBie?

Keith's insight from the Lonely Seat

I guess the thing that stands out for me in this chapter is that essentially, this is a selling exercise, a very formal and structured one, but a selling exercise, nevertheless. Ali speaks of answering the question and addressing the issues and concerns of the client.

In any selling environment, it's all too easy to keep going on about benefit "B" and benefit "C" and benefit "D", just because we want to show off how good we are when all the client is interested in is benefit "A" because that is where their problem lies. Once you have addressed benefit "A" unless they ask; SHUT UP! Or you run the risk of complicating matters.

The storyboard methodology Ali has mentioned is used in the world of film production, giving a structure and framework into which the detail can be added piece by piece. Going through it step by step.

That helps to engage your whole team in the process by letting them see how the part they are working on fits into the whole picture. So that's another big win for staff engagement.

One final point... If your prospect sees that it's not just one person trying to sell to them but a whole team fully engaged in the project, then you will be streets ahead of the competition.

Beach of Gold

CHAPTER 9: FACING THE INQUISITION

Introduction

In some cases, there may be a final bid stage after you have I submitted your proposal; this is the 'Interview Stage'.

A shortlist of bidders may be asked to make a presentation or be interviewed by the procurement team. What might that entail?

Interview Preparation

In most cases, you will be invited via email or through a message on the tendering portal to attend an interview at a specific time or place (or possibly online). Whatever the time and place specified, make it a priority, it doesn't look good if you try to change the time or place!

You should be given an outline of what is expected, possibly a list of questions and an outline of any timings and presentation elements the client is looking for. It is unlikely that you will be advised as to who you will be meeting, but if you do know, then look them up on LinkedIn to see what you can find out.

Whatever the client is asking you to talk about or questions they need answering, remember these key points in developing your presentation or responses:

1. Make everything relevant to the bid and the problem that your proposed solution will address. Specifically, how it will benefit the client.

2. Have evidence prepared. They will almost certainly ask you about your previous experience in delivering contracts such as the one you are bidding for. You could take printed case studies in with you, but at least be prepared to talk about your previous experience with specific details.

3. Don't overdo the PowerPoint! Keep it clean and simple.

Building Confidence for Post-Submission Meetings

Standing in front of an evaluation panel, talking about your proposal, and answering questions can be nerve-racking. The key here is to *'know your stuff'*.

Once you have developed your presentation/evidence/notes for the session, then practice. Get the people together who will be presenting and make sure that you all know exactly what the proposal says and how you are going to answer any questions asked. If you know your stuff, your nerves will be much less than if you go in unprepared.

In terms of the people who should attend a post-submission interview, make sure whoever is the dedicated point of contact for the contract is there. Only send people who know the bid, the answers to the questions and who will be working on the contract.

The evaluators don't want to see the managing director. They want to see the people who will be on the ground delivering the work.

This interview can often be about who they want to work with, and that comes down to both expertise and personality, so bear that in mind. Interview scoring can sometimes be a little less objective than proposal scoring.

In essence, know your stuff, prepare a presentation/ question answers that relate specifically to the proposal and the problem that needs solving, select the right people to attend and when you have it nailed down; practice, practice, practice...

Keith's insight from the Lonely Seat

Ali quite rightly talks about "knowing your stuff". In this chapter. I would take it a stage further than that.

Perhaps you already know it, but I will say it anyway! I always feel that once we get to this stage, the decision will not be based on hard, cold facts. As Ali said, this stage can be more subjective than the previous stage. The ace you carry can be summed up in one word..." *CONFIDENCE".*

Most managing directors are confident that they can deliver, but as Ali said, it may not be the managing director the client wants to be talking to; it is the delivery team, the ones who will see the project through to completion. Are they confident in the company's abilities, in their own abilities? Truly confident? Should even the faintest hint that confidence is lacking be picked up on, chances are the bid will be lost.

If I were talking to your delivery team in advance of that meeting, I would be reassuring them that it is they, themselves, who are the prize! They have the ability to deliver a solution that will bring exactly what the client needs with minimum stress. If you like, a 'fit and forget' solution.

Beach of Gold

Beach of Gold

CHAPTER 10: THE JOURNEY TOWARDS PERFECTION

Introduction

There is no such thing as the perfect bid. However, you can develop strategies, learn skills, create collateral and develop processes that will make each one better than the last.

Throughout this book, we have taken you through much of what you need to know to get out there and start your journey towards winning work through bidding for public and private sector tenders. The cycle of activity your business will adopt based on this learning is:

Continuous Improvement in Bidding Strategies

Of course, things change all the time. What might work today may not work tomorrow. It is, therefore, vital that as part of your bidding strategy, you continue to analyse feedback from your submissions, good and bad, to ensure that you are always approaching your proposal development in the most effective way.

Think about the people you have developing your proposals.

Are they the right people? Do they have the skills? Could you source training to help upskill them? At Kindridge, we have developed a bespoke online modular self-directed course to help you and your workforce develop winning bids. You can access it here:

https://alibagleycoach.samcart.com/products/an-introduction-to-bidding

Adapting to Changing Landscapes

In recent years, we have seen a huge increase in the requirement for evidence of social value, environmental sustainability and responsibility measures. Statistical evidence is now more important for high scores than stories and case studies.

Stay aware of these trends and changes and make sure that you continually update your lessons learned and capture planning information to support your ability to develop outstanding bids.

CONCLUSION

Bidding for work is a necessary activity for growing your business. It enables you to win contracts that secure your short-and long-term revenue. There are many opportunities out there in the public and private sectors and all you have to do is find them, bid for them and win them.

Ok, it's not quite that simple, as you will know if you have read through this book. But the opportunities are there. The ability to learn the skills required is literally in your hands. And if, having read through this book and maybe taken our training course, you think, to hell with it, let's get the professionals in. You know where we are.

To paraphrase Nanny McPhee:

> *'When you need us but do not want us, we are there for you. When you want us but no longer need us, then we have done what we set out to do.'*

In essence, as we work with you, we upskill you and build your collateral so that, eventually you can do it by yourself. But we will still be there when you need to be covered for absence or just because you know that nobody does it better . . .

A final word from the Lonely Seat . . .

"If business was easy, everyone would have one." That's been my catchphrase for more years than I would like to remember. I guess it's a cliché, but that doesn't rob it of its value.

The world is full of people spouting their opinions and claiming that when the time is right, they will be setting up in business for themselves to show the world how it is done. But the thing is, when push comes to shove, the right time never seems to come.

Business does not come to us; we have to chase it. We have to put ourselves out there and risk the rejections and failures if we are going to stand a chance of success. If we don't join the race, how will we ever win it?

Go for it. Just remember, excitement starts at the edge of the diving board!

Beach of Gold

ABOUT THE AUTHORS

Ali Bagley is a bid specialist, able to both manage and craft winning written responses to tenders in both the public and private sectors.

Originally from a corporate bid management background in infrastructure, Ali now works with clients who need expert support in winning work that will sustain and grow their businesses.

She is also a best-selling author of business support books, a radio show host on Big Ear Radio with her show, 'Write Up Your Ali' and a writers' coach, helping budding authors to develop business books which deliver solutions to their readers' challenges.

Ali approaches bidding and bid training with a can-do attitude, a proven technique for developing winning responses and a stress busting sense of humour.

She is a wife, mum to 4 kids and grandma to 6 more. And she loves stories and solving puzzles . . .

Keith Trubshaw is a serial entrepreneur, long-standing occupant of the 'Lonely Seat' and an expert in supporting business growth.

He has been where you are, he knows the pressures and the sacrifices business leaders make in pursuit of success.

In his book, The Lonely Seat, Keith tells us about his journey in business, the ups, the downs and the lessons learned (or not sometimes!). It's a great read and shows us that no matter what is thrown at you, there are always choices and hopefully more bright days than dark.

Keith may not know much about the technical ins and outs of developing good bids, but, by golly, he can tell a story. His advice, for those of you sitting in that Lonely Seat, striving daily to grow your businesses and meet all your responsibilities, in seeing the bigger picture for business growth, just had to be included in this book.

He is a Husband and Dad to 2 kids.

And he loves music, playing guitar and being on stage . . .

Beach of Gold

Appendices

Resources and Tools

A Typical Storyboard Template

Bid Title	Name of the bid this question belongs to
Question Number / Section	i.e. Quality Response Question 3.1
Weighting / Score	The weighting / score available for this response
Format Constraints	i.e. font type/size, margins, background, highlighting etc.
Owner	The person responsible for developing the response
1st Draft Deadline	Date that initial outline / bullets must be completed by
Final Draft Deadline	Date that a full final draft must be completed by
Storyboarding sections	
Introduction:	Provide a brief introduction to the technical question. Clearly state the problem or requirement you are addressing.

Context and Background:	*Provide context to the question. Include any relevant background information that helps the evaluator understand your response more clearly.*
Objective:	*Clearly state the objective or goal of your response. Define what you aim to achieve in addressing the question, the solution, features and benefits.*
Methodology:	*Outline the approach or methodology you will use to answer the question. Break down the steps or stages involved in your approach.*

Technical Details:	*Present the technical details relevant to the question. Use diagrams, charts, or graphs to illustrate complex concepts. Include relevant data, calculations, or specifications.*
Risk Mitigation:	*Address any potential risks associated with your approach/ solution. Explain how you plan to mitigate these risks.*
Innovation / Added Value:	*Highlight any innovative aspects of your solution. Clearly articulate the value your solution brings to the project.*

Timeline:	Provide a visual timeline or schedule for the implementation of your solution. Break down the project into phases or milestones.
Resources:	Specify the resources required to implement your solution (personnel, equipment, materials). Include a breakdown of costs if applicable/ not already in the pricing submission.
Quality Assurance and Testing:	Explain how you will ensure the quality of your solution. Detail any testing processes or quality control measures.
Compliance and Standards:	Demonstrate how your solution complies with relevant industry standards or regulations. Highlight any certifications or qualifications that support your approach.

Conclusion:	*Summarise the key points of your response. Reiterate how your solution effectively addresses the requirements of the question.*
Appendices:	*Where allowed, include any additional supporting documents, technical specifications, or references. Attach relevant visuals, such as photographs, charts, or diagrams.*
Each section should flow logically, providing a comprehensive, relevant and persuasive response to the technical question posed in the bid.	

Case Studies

A Typical Case Study template

Contract:		
Client:		**Insert picture from the delivery here**
Date From-To:		
Contract Value:		
Key Contact in Client Organisation:		
Key Requirements:	1. 2. 3.	
Outputs achieved:	1. 2. 3.	
Outcomes Achieved:	1. 2. 3.	

Our Solution / Methodology / Actions:	
Testimonials:	1. 2. 3.
Lessons Learned:	1. 2. 3.

There's a beach of Gold Just Around the Corner

ISBN: 9781738535828

Printed in Great Britain
by Amazon

43215614R00086